THE ALL NEW STYLE OF MAGAZINE-BOOKS

SDM LIVE ®

www.SDMLIVE.com

MP

MOCY PUBLISHING
WWW.MOCYPUBLISHING.COM

Katrina Carson

180
of my Life

ALL NEW EPISODE COMING SOON!

SDM LIVE ®

EDITOR-IN-CHIEF
D. "Casino" Bailey
casino@sdmlive.com

EDITORIAL DIRECTOR
Sheree Cranford
sheree@sdmlive.com

GRAPHIC/WEB DESIGNER
D. "Casino" Bailey
casino@sdmlive.com

ACCOUNT EXECUTIVE
Katrina Carson
kartina@sdmlive.com

PHOTOGRAPHERS
Anterlon Terrell Fritz
Treagen Colston
Terance Drake

CONTRIBUTORS
Katrina Carson
No'el Snyder

COPY ORDERS & ADVERTISING OFFICE
Send Money Order or Check to:
Mocy Publishing
P.O. Box 35195
Detroit, Michigan 48235
(833) 736-5483
advertise@sdmlive.com

Copy Order Item
SDM Live Magazine Issue #20
S&H Plus Retail Price - $9.99 per copy

WWW.SDMLIVE.COM

Printed by CreateSpace, An Amazon.com Company

MP
MOCY PUBLISHING

Copyright © 2018 SDM NETWORK LLC,
a division of Mocy Publishing, LLC and
C'Cliche, LLC. All rights reserved.
Printed in the U.S.A.

ISSUE 20 - 2018
CONTENTS

pg. 12
WILLIE FINKLEA
AnueYou Global owner and founder taking his brand to the top.

pg. 16
WEDDING KINGS
The midwest party/wedding promoters switching up the game of entertainment.

pg. 20
KFIRE
Inspiring people through her godly movement with Horns & Halos.

pg.23
TOP 10 CHARTS
The hottest albums and digital singles this month features Ella Mai, KFire Queen Naija and more.

1

Rocketfish™ - 4-Port 4K HDMI Switch Box - Black
$79.99
www.bestbuy.com

2

Logitech - Harmony Ultimate One 15-Device Universal Remote - Black
$59.99
www.bestbuy.com

3

Facebook - 10.1" Portal with Alexa - Video Calling - White
$199.99
www.bestbuy.com

LET'S TALK WITH

Katrina Carson

ANUEYOU
GLOBAL RADIO

SDM LIVE
UNPLUGGED

TUNE IN AND LISTEN TO LET'S TALK WITH KATRINA CARSON EVERY MONDAY FROM 6PM - 7PM

AS SHE GIVES YOU AN EXCLUSIVE BACKSTAGE PASS TO THE LATEST ENTERTAINMENT NEWS.

WWW.ANUEYOUMEDIA.COM

Let's Rock & Roll

THE 2019 HALL OF FAME CANDIDATES ARE IN. AND ICE CUBE GETS STAR ON HOLLYWOOD WALK OF FAME AND TAKES A PHOTO WITH THE OLD NWA CREW.
by Cheraee C.

What iconic artist would you like to see inducted into the 2019 Rock & Roll Hall of Fame? Voting has begun online and in person at the Museum of Rock & Roll in Cleveland, Ohio. The ballot is very tough including a mixture of new and old artists who have and haven't been on the ballot before. Artists like LL Cool J, Janet Jackson, Rufus featuring Chaka Khan, Radiohead, John Prine, Def Leppard, Devo, Rage Against the Machine, Roxy Music, and a few others.

For an artist to even be eligible for the Rock & Roll Hall of Fame, they had to release their first project at least 25 years prior to the year of their nomination. The inductees are going to be announced in December 2018, and the actual induction ceremony is going to be in March 2019 held in Brooklyn, New York. This event is sponsored by Klipsch Audio, which is a leading speaker and headphone manufacturer, and an strategic partner and sponsor for the Rock & Roll Hall of Fame.

THE HOTTEST RADIO SHOWS ON THE PLANET!

DOWNLOAD THE APPS

SDM Live, AnueYou Global Radio or iHeart Radio today!

AnueYou Going Global

BUSINESS OWNER WILLIE FINKLEA IS CLIMBING TO THE TOP WITH HIS COMPANY BRAND ANUEYOU GLOBAL AND MEDIA NETWORK.

by Cheraee C.

Q. Tell us briefly about your brand, what your name means, and what is your company mission.

A. Our company brand is Anueyou Global and the name Anueyou is an ancient Hebrew name meaning (One God, The Almighty, The Most High). We feel with the creator and the creations working together, there is nothing holding you back from ever accomplishing your dreams. Our company's mission is to inspire and empower individuals to reach their full potential by educating them about lifestyle changes, health & wealth education and financial literacy.

Q. What is the backstory behind your health and wellness drinks and how did the recipes for them come about?

A. The story behind the drinks began from a relative of mine who had the honor of traveling abroad and lived in Africa for approximately twenty years. Upon one of her visits to the United States, we were introduced to a ginger drink recipe that she used while in Africa. From then, another family took the recipe and opened up a family business featuring a drink called "Greta's Ginger Guice." Many years later, I decided to come out with another line of healthy drinks which included, Ginger, Moringa, Tumeric, and Beet drinks.

Q. How much do you sell your products for, how can customers purchase them, and what made you want to market them the way you do?

A. Our business operates through entrepreneur development with a Multi-Level Marketing structure. We strive on developing and strengthening leaders because personal growth and development is essential to being successful. We chose this way of direct marketing so that every individual could take advantage of an opportunity to live their dreams. Our prices and membership packages are listed on the website…. Anueyouglobal. com

Q. You also have TV and radio platforms. Tell us briefly what made you want to start a TV/radio station and when did you start these businesses?

A. Anueyou Global also operates a TV and media platform. Our television platform can be downloaded on Roku and smart television devices. Our radio platform can be downloaded from your smartphone app store or I-phone. We started these platforms so that we could reach a broader audience and educate them through audio and visual learning. These platforms empower each one of our business partners to be able to operate business from the palm of their hand. This allows us to be in any living room throughout the country and internationally at any time of the day. Therefore, business partners and customers are able to educate themselves about our company and what we have to offer at their own convenience.

Q. How can a person launch a radio/TV show on your network and what type of packages are you offering?

A. Anueyou Global media offers other individuals the opportunity to share information on Health/Wellness, financial literacy, education, or any other aspect that promotes a positive change or lifestyle. All of this is done through our business partner SDM Live. All inquires to these networks can be obtained by accessing anueyou-media.com. Click on the contact page and submit your information.

Q. As far as branding goes, what are your current strategies for expanding your TV and radio station?

A. Our current strategies for expanding and branding our television and radio networks is to connect with other positive partners such as SDM Live and their affiliates and having experienced producers and broadcasters. We are so excited about our very first talk show program hosted by none other than professional recording artist Katrina Carson. The show's title is "Let's Talk with Katrina Carson." We will have an array of shows that will air and be posted on our website daily. In closing, we wish each and every individual success and we hope that you reach your dreams and maybe just maybe on this journey we will cross paths to share positive experiences and life changes.

Art Is Life

ARTIST CHASTNEY "CHAZ" CONLEY IS ALL ABOUT SPREADING THE BEAUTY OF ART THROUGH BODYPAINTING, TRAP PAINTING, AND SKIN WARS EVENTS IN METRO DETROIT.
by Cheraee C.

Q. So Chaz, you have an upcoming event on body art. What made you want to do this type of event?

A. I was always a fan of Skin Wars (the TV show). That's when I started bodypainting. I began to become exposed to artists I had never seen before. In knowing that Detroit has so much talent that goes unrecognized, I figured who needs to go to L.A. Let's create the competition right here at home.

Q. Why are you so intrigued by bodypainting and how do you feel like it affects people?

A. Bodypainting allows those who are having body complex issues, or who have scars, or those who are just introverts an opportunity to be free. To be liberated… yet covered at the same time.

Q. What made you want to host this event on Sweetest Day?

A. I initially wanted it to be on the weekend of Halloween. However, the venue was booked. When I noticed the date available was Sweetest Day, I was excited to give people an alternative to traditional events. Sweetest Day is about love.. and love provokes sensuality. The human body is key to sensuality and should be celeberated.

Q. Tell us about your business and what you think about the rise of painting and sipping events? Have you ever been to one of those events?

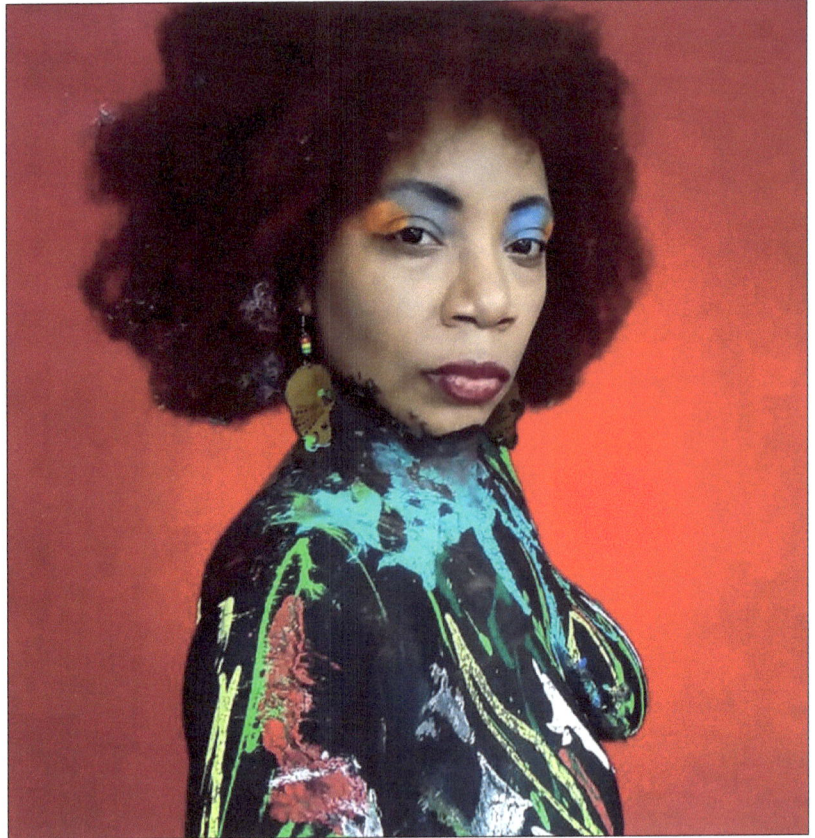

A. I actually have my own company called "The Art of Life LLC." It started as me hosting my own Painting with Chaz mobile paint party service which I currently still do. People seem to be more creative when they have a few cocktails. Lol, and music and art go hand in hand because it sends vibrations to the core and then the core responds through rhythm and movement, which coincidentally are two principles of design. I have not been to trap and paint though, well not yet, lol.

Q. Do you think art is on the rise in general and which type of art do you think appeals to the people the most?

A. I do believe art is on the rise because people are looking for healthy ways to express themselves. And also where entrepreneurship lies, lies the creative thinker. You have to be able to think outside of the box in any business. You now see not only entrepreneurs, but corporations participating in art forms as team builders. Contemporary Art would have to be the most popular as it is the art that came about in the 20th century. Not to mention Performing Arts where people are displaying their creativity on canvas or through self-expression in front of a live audience.

She's Cold as I.C.E.

RAPPER I.C.E. IS AN UPCOMING FEMALE MC REPRESENTED BY THE BMR MOVEMENT AND IS STRIVING TO MAKE HER NAME A STAPLE IN THE MUSIC INDUSTRY.

by Cheraee C.

Q. Artists names tell a lot about themselves. Is it any specific meaning or story behind your name?

A. As a child growing up I was a huge fan of Detroit artists like Blade Icewood. I loved his music, and the attention he grabbed when he walked through the door. I knew one day I wanted to be just like him. Just the female version! So when I begin rapping I was like call me ICE!

Q. How did you enjoy your experience at the 2018 SDMLive Awards? Would you perform again next year?

A. My experience at the 2018 SDMLive awards was great and different from the underground performances that I normally do. It was great talking and mingling with other dope artists. I also really enjoyed being on a big stage in front of a big audience. It gave me a taste of what's to come.

Q. Many female artists are mothers. How do you balance motherhood and music?

A. Well I handle my music and my children the same. They're both my BABIES! With the help of my family (immediate family members/managers/record label) and God, all things are possible. Let's just say, I don't leave them in hands that I wouldn't trust with my life or as my own!

Q. What is your mission as a female rapper in the music industry? How do you plan to change the female side of the rap game?

A. My mission is to give the industry my all, 110%.! I want to start off by saying the women in the game right now is killing it, But I plan on making the people love me, giving them something new, something they have never seen and something fresh!

Q. How do you feel about all the female industry beef going on between Cardi B and Nicki Minaj? Do you favor one artist over the other?

A. Honestly, I don't feel anything towards it. I'm an outsider looking in. I really don't know what's going on with the two, and personally it has nothing to do with I.C.E., and no, I don't favor one over the other. I think they both are dope in their own way!

Q. Do you have any upcoming shows, projects, or albums coming out?

A. Yes, I have a lot of bookings where I will be opening up for some of the dopest artists. Sep. 29 with Lil Boosie, Oct 6 with Tekashi 6ix9ine, my very own showcase "SO COLD SHOWCASE" Oct. 27 where alot of dope artists will be attending, including my team BMR. Oct.28, with Chief Keef. Also, I'm working on my EP, I'm putting together for all my fans!

Meet The Wedding Kings

TWO OF THE MOST PROMINENT WEDDING DJS IN MICHIGAN ARE
STEADY RAISING THE BAR FOR MOBILE DEJAYING.

by Cheraee C.

Q. What is The Commission? Who are the members in it and who started it?

A. The Commission no longer exists and I started it with DJ Hollyhood and another guy DJ K Redd.
We eventually added a final member, DJ Baby Boy. The group was put together to maintain dominance on the mobile DJ side of things. I get so booked that I have to turn a lot of events down, so I figured if I created a group of guys I can depend on, I could shoot that business to them. Laziness, disloyalty, and greed killed the group before we could even get going good.

Q. What made you guys change your name to the Wedding Kings and will you guys be recruiting new members?

A. We dropped the other two members and became Wedding Kingz. We chose that name because that's our focus and specialty. We don't care about bars or clubs. There's no money in that. Weddings are where the money is and we are at the top as it relates to who people call when they want their weddings done right. Nah, we won't be adding anyone. It'll just be me and DJ Hollyhood.

Q. What made you guys become so invested and crafty with wedding dejaying out of all the type of events you can dj?

A. Weddings are where the money is and it's where you can truly display your craft. At weddings, you have to entertain a crowd from ages 1-100. So, you have to put that perfect balance to your mix and make sure everyone enjoys themselves. That's a tough task, but one we relish every week. Clubs, it's typically one age group or a smaller range to where you can play one genre or one style and get through the night. There's no challenge in that.

Q. Describe the djs who were at your weddings when you guys got married. On a scale from 1-10 we're they good or bad? What's y'all wedding story?

A. I didn't even have a DJ, I rented a stereo system from Rent-A-Center, and burned some cd's! Lol! This was in 2004, well before I became a DJ. I didn't even know any DJ's at the time. I think DJ Hollyhood got married in Vegas by a Elvis Presley impersonator. Of course now my wife wants a huge wedding for our 20th year anniversary.

Q. From a DJ perspective, do weddings have a slow or peak season because it seems like weddings and nuptials are always trending, but wedding dates are pretty similar.

A. The wedding season kind of slows down from Nov-Jan for me. I still have one or two during that timeframe, but nothing like when the season starts in March, where we'll do 10-12 weddings a month at times. Wedding season use to be like April-Sept, but the millennials are changing that standard.

Q. What is the strangest day or holiday one of y'all couples got married on and had a reception?

A. The night before Thanksgiving...that's a black holiday! Lol! Every black woman in America is cooking on that night. Needless to say, the crowd wasn't big to begin with and they left early. It was a total waste. I also had a wedding on Valentine's Day. It was a way for a guy to take his girl to the wedding and have a cheap date since the food and liquor were free! Lol! But, I guess a lot of women wasn't having it because that wedding was dead too. I don't even take weddings, or any event for that matter on holidays anymore.

Q. Describe one of your favorite wedding venues, and one of your favorite couples that you serviced?

A. My all time favorite venue is Queen's Palace in Allen Park. This place is beautiful. It just so happens to be owned by this female Arabic DJ that I use to give DJ lessons to. She's like the biggest Arabic DJ in Michigan. My favorite couples are the couples who save up to pay for my services. They're much more appreciative. The clients that are more affluent or their parents are paying for the wedding tend to be the more difficult clients.

Q. Are the Wedding Kings booked up for 2020 yet seeing people are always booking you guys?

A. We have a few weddings on the books for 2020, but we are about 95% booked up for 2019. Its bananas how much love we get. If we're booked, people will change their wedding dates to get us. We've had brides have nervous breakdowns because we're booked on their dream date. We are the guys you want to call if you're getting married. There are a few clowns out there that have bit my style, or I personally showed them the way on how to do weddings, but they don't compare because we're constantly changing the way we do things. We don't want your wedding to just be a formality; We want it to be an experience where your guests are there looking forward to what's next.

Q. How does it feel to be gracing the cover of this SDM-Live Magazine?

A. We're super excited about just being in the magazine to begin with. Being on the cover is the icing on the cake. There are thousands of DJ's in the metro area, but we've worked hard and invested so much time and money into our businesses that it feels good to be recognized. Congrats to my bro DJ Hollyhood for winning DJ of the year too!

Q. Describe a DJ world without the Wedding Kings?

A. They'd be in the stone ages without us. No one here cared about presentation until we started doing it. Now it's gone viral. I started it and my bro DJ Hollyhood was right there with me, so naturally he got into it and we just took off. There's not one DJ that has stepped his or her presentation and lighting game up that can say I didn't directly or indirectly influence it. That's allowed DJ's to eat better because it allowed them to charge more. The more we raise our prices, the more another DJ can eat better by raising their prices. This mobile DJ game is ours. We set the market for it. If we lowered our prices, it would be a lot of DJ's out of work.

The Heat is Getting Hotter...
TEKASHI 69 GETS BUSTED BY FEDS!
by Katrina Carson

Tekashi69, hiphop star's manager and 2 other associates that were just fired from his team are in federal custody after getting busted on racketeering charges. As of right now, we are unsure of the fate of Tekashi 69 when it comes to this matter. Law enforcement sources are saying that he was recently arrested by ATF agents in New York City.

According to sources, they all could be facing racketeering and firearms charges. Tekashi 69 has a new project coming out soon, however his fans are more concerened with whats happening with his case. As of right now, it is not looking too good. However, some may agree with the saying, "all publicity is good publicity"!

Plenty Horns & Plenty Halos

FEMALE ARTIST KFIRE IS BRINGING A NEW SOULFUL SOUND, INSPIRED BY GOD AND IS HERE TO INSPIRE PEOPLE THROUGH HER GODLY MOVEMENT.

by No'el Snyder.

Q. In May, you released your first album, Horns and Halos. The album was courageously uplifting as it displayed praise. For those who haven't obtained the opportunity to give it a listen, could you elaborate on the meaning you conveyed on the album?

A. On "Horns and Halos" I wanted to get several messages across. The primary story is the internal fight we all have within ourselves. Some people don't want to admit it, but all of us have a conscience but we try to mask it with our own justifications. I believe that urge to do the right thing comes from God. The hard part is no matter what, it is a battle. The Horns are the evil I have been exposed to growing up or wrong things that are in me naturally. For example, your father might have been addicted to alcohol and maybe you didn't grow up around him but you have that same struggle. That would represent Horns -a vice or wickedness that you want to try and defeat, or you gave up on fighting. In this project, I'm pushing us to fight. Halos represent the things that God has placed in you that you may be naturally good at (God-given gifts) or traits that are Godly such as patience, compassion etc. It also represents the non-materialistic things in your life that bring you joy; more so, the situations and people that God placed in your life can bring you joy.

Q. Could you tell the readers about a real-life occurrence that altered your perception used as inspiration to help create Horns and Halos?

A. There was a lot of personal experiences that inspired this album but one, in particular, was my interactions with one of my older cousins. I always looked up to him and saw him as a big brother. I remember when I was younger, I thought he was the coolest person, period! I didn't get to be around him as much as I wanted because he stayed in another state. To make the long story short, I was in my early twenties; he came back around and I noticed that his mindset was different from mine. He would manipulate and con people to get what he wanted out of them. I remember I started taking rapping seriously, and he started becoming jealous of me; not because I was doing something he couldn't do, but he could see I was choosing a different lifestyle and he couldn't influence me the way he used to when we were younger. He would tell me how he respected what I do, but it wasn't his lane. In this album, I touch on why I may have made some of the mistakes I did in my past, but ultimately I realized we all have the power of choice. We have free will, which means at some point we can't blame anyone but ourselves. "Horns and Halos" is all about my choices, the choices of people around me, and how I was influenced by those choices. There were many experiences I had with people that helped inspire the theme throughout the album.

Q. I've been seeing your album frequently all over social media. In what other ways have you maintained the relevance of Horns and Halos in these past four months?

A. Wow! To be honest, I recognize that's all God. I would post stuff on social media, but I have had people reach out to me from all over because somehow they heard the music. I believe marketing strategies are dope, but that's not what has been keeping my album relevant. It's simply because God is making connections to people who genuinely enjoy the music and the message and they are sharing it. I'm grateful for that.

Q. Is there anyone that you want to work within your city of Detroit as far as features and production?

A. As far as production, I have one of the greatest producers. Throne Muzik is very gifted and he is also my husband. I love what we have going on as a team. I never was the type of artist to just work with a lot of producers especially when I have great chemistry with one. Maybe on future projects, it could happen if it fits. There is a lot of talent in the city so you never know. When it comes to features, most of the time I have to click with the person outside of music before we do a song together. Talent doesn't move me as much as character and work ethic so we'll see. I know Dre Breeze just to name one, but there are some other artists too. That's Godspeed I prefer letting things fall into place.

Q. Recently, you recorded a new song titled, Victory, which was lyrically dressed and compacted with uplifting lyrics. Can us listeners anticipate more music on the way or an upcoming EP?

A. That is a good question. I do plan on letting this project breathe a bit, so after I drop that single digitally (Victory), I'm going to rest from releasing music. That's the plan for now.

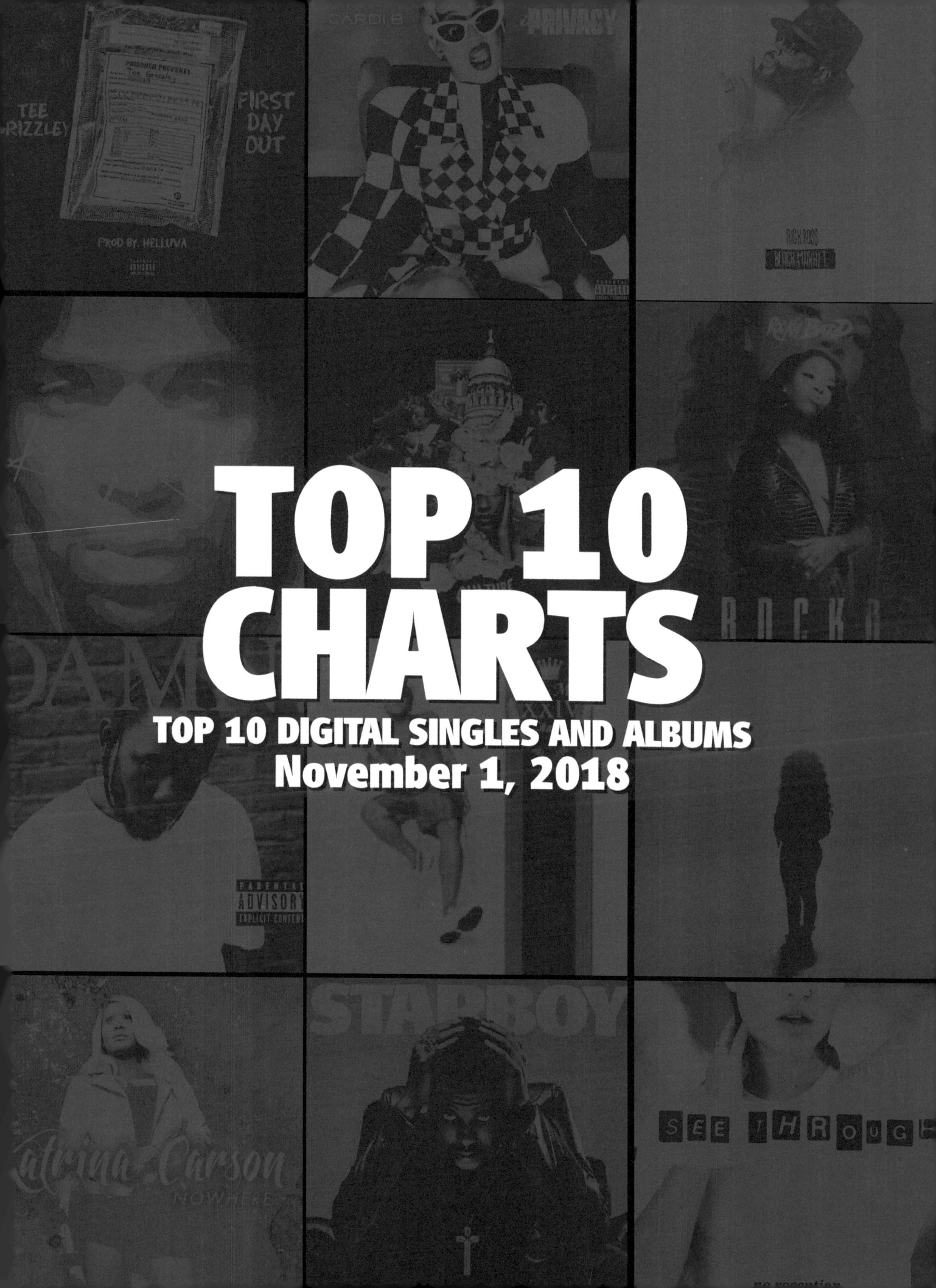

TOP 10 CHARTS

TOP 10 DIGITAL SINGLES AND ALBUMS
November 1, 2018

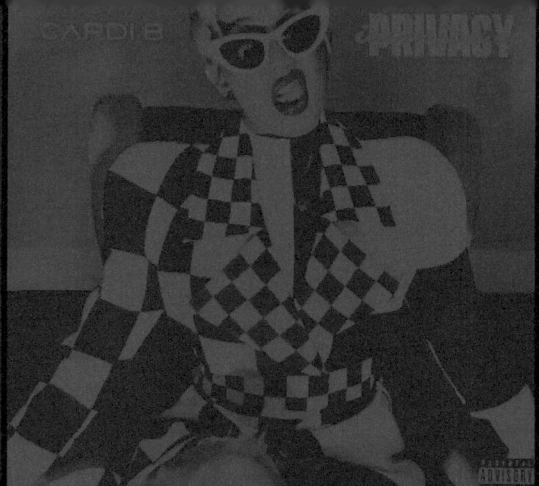

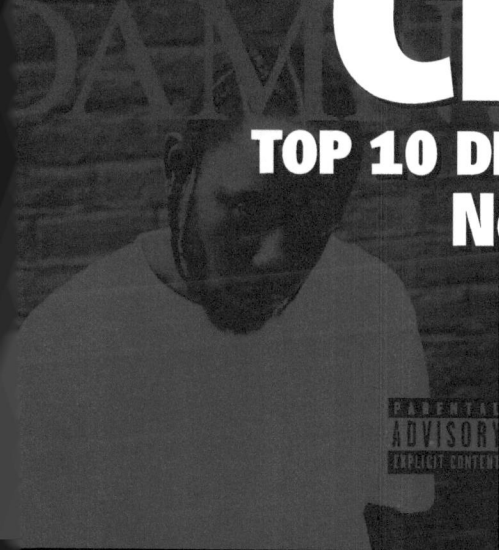

TOP 10 CHARTS

ELLA MAI PERFORMING LIVE WITH HER HIT SINGLE "BOO'D UP" AND "TRIP" ON "SNL".

TOP #1

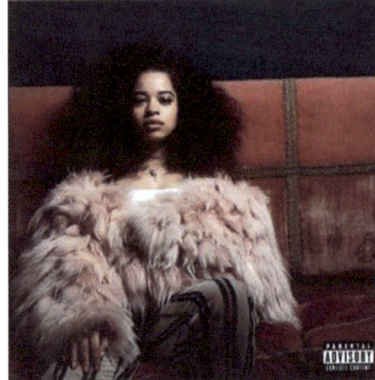

Ella Mai
Ella Mai

An R&B sensation Ella Mai drops a new self-titled ablum filled with hits excutive produced by Dj Mustard.

TOP 10 SINGLES CHART OF THE MONTH

No.	Artist - Song Title
1	ELLA MAI - TRIP
2	CARDI B - MONEY
3	TYGA - TASTE
4	KATRINA CARSON - NOWHERE
5	DRAKE - NON STOP
6	KING DILLON - SUPER DRIP
7	LIL WAYNE - UPROAR
8	LIL DUVAL - SMILE FT. SNOOP DOGG AND BALL GREEZY
9	YELLA BEZZY - THAT'S ON ME
10	DION PRICE - NOVACANE

TOP 10 ALBUMS CHART OF THE MONTH

No.	Artist - Album Title
1	ELLA MAI - ELLA MAI
2	LIL WAYNE - THA CARTER III
3	QUEEN NAIJA - QUEEN NAIJA
4	KING DILLON - THIRTY-ONE-THREE
5	NIKKI MINAJ - QUEEN
6	DRAKE - SCORPION
7	CARDI B - INVASION OF PRIVACY
8	DION PRICE - HEART OF A LION
9	MIGOS - CULTURE II
10	H.E.R. - H.E.R.

Horns & Halos
ARTIST: KFIRE
RATING: 5

Horns and Halos introduces the battling theme of good and evil/angels versus demons as the young music artist locates balance, after allowing christ to enter her life. Within the Detroit artist lyrics, K. Fire struggles with her family not believing in her goals, which results in the repercussions of her seeking approval through the different types of males she's encounted. As society hurdles negativity, K. Fire stumbles upon the situations that were never resolved within herself. Now she's focused on her faults and making her weaknesses her strengths. The varied, production was mostly done by Throne Muzik, with additional production from Ravo, and Verbatum. These instrumentals were fully compelling, powerful, and enjoyably solid. One of the tracks that stood out to my ears was titled Grateful. This track urges us to have a spirit of gratitude, with appreciation of it all no matter the negative or positive. This track also offers assistance in reflection on what God has done for ones life. With soulful features from Gerard Brooks and Paris Simone that set the tone for the album and an amazing verse from Lance Hitch on the track titled, Crown, K. Fire's delivery was extremely eloquent, which gave a confident approach towards all ten tracks, making this LP a classic hip-hop album with it being structured so well. The absolute best part about Horns and Halos was that there wasn't a single usuage of profanity within her lyrics, and that's truly a rarity in the music genre of hip-hop. Be sure to check out K. Fire's debut album Horns and Halos on ITunes, Google Play, and Spotify. Links provided below.

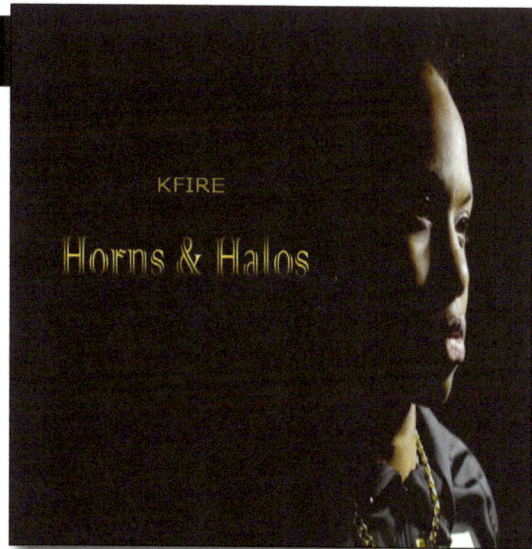

See Through
ARTIST: No Reception
RATING: 4

I've been invested in the music genre of hip-hop over these past few months, but recently, I acquired a punk/rock music project that provided delicate vocals of strength, alongside raging lyrics of appreciation. No Reception graces us listeners with her one woman, punk rock EP, See Through.

The nineteen-year-old songwriter sonically lures us music lovers into the subconscious mind of an artist whose self-reflection outshines the production on this four-track EP. Doing a hundred percent of the instrument playing and songwriting, we listeners obtain a glimpse into the woman behind these soothing, chaotic vocals. No Reception provides transparent lyrics that are strongly dedicated to her loved ones, who, on any occasion, she was unconditionally present for, but as the time approached for them to reciprocate the similar benefits of support and love, they proved unable. This provoked No Receptions' decision to isolate herself from the people who've taken advantage of her love and kindness, as she buries herself into "do not disturb" mode throughout See Through. The talented New York native greatly integrates thrash, melodic singing, subtle percussive guitar strings, and bass, with subversive drum strikes to the cymbals we hear throughout this short collection of tracks. Songs such as Door Mat and Can't Be Fixed supply an aggressive, thunderous rhythm, rendering a strong affirmation towards the lyrics. The track Losing Myself To You offers a pleasant guitar melody that provides a blissful intermix with her shrieking vocals, making this track a fan favorite for a strong sensation of solace with a calming release. No Reception delivers a star-studded performance that awards consistency and conviction for her vengeful, pulsating lyrics. Check out No Reception's debut EP, See Through on all digital streaming services, and also check out the visuals for no receptions. single, Time To Kill via YouTube. Links provided below.

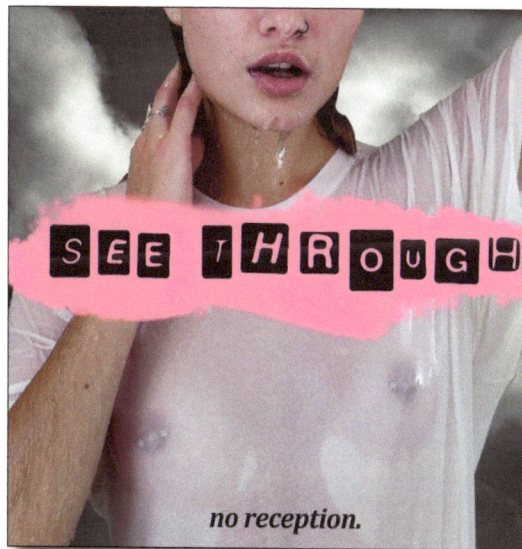

HEELS &
SKILLZ

Nona Malone
is a beautiful model
from Houston, TX.

instagram
@nonamalone313

Photography by
@barearmy

Gaggy Sky

A sexy model
from Detroit MI.

instagram
@missgabbysky

HEELS &
SKILLZ

Photography by
@barearmy

Kendra Kouture

A video and runway
model from Muskegon, MI.

instagram
@kouture_world

Cheraee's Corner

WHY DO PEOPLE LACK A REAL VISION FOR THEIR CAREERS AND SUCCESS?

by Cheraee C.

It's nothing wrong with having a dream or being multi-talented, but we live in an era of redundancy and competition. Everybody is trying to do the same thing in the same industry just a little differently. Somebody might have more connections, a bigger fanbase, more money or etc then the other person. The reality is Hollywood isn't for everybody and everybody isn't going to be rich or famous.

If I'm going to dedicate myself to something, it's going to be something I plan to do forever through trial and error. People are steady investing into careers that aren't worth the investment. We can't just think temporarily, we have to think longterm. By all means do what you love, but why not do something bigger, better, and more fruitful? Like they say, "don't let the money make you, you make the money."

NEXT 2 BLOW

YOVNG RAH

Q. Tell the readers about yourself, and how you plan on making an impact in the music industry.

A. I go by the name Yovng Rah, I'm 20 years old, and I've been a music addict for 20 years lol. Since a young age, I've always been a writer, from poetry to books to essays.. the pen was my passion. The message I want people to receive through my music is no matter what color, race, gender, rich, poor; no matter your situation do whatever you want, live your life, and don't change for anybody... One life.

Q. Tell the readers why they should take the time out to listen to your music. What makes your lyrics notable?

A. I feel like people should listen to my music because I'm very versatile and make songs for everyone. I make songs that will open your mind to think, some you can turn up off of, and for the strippers to make some money off of. My lyrics are notable because I can make someone cry from connecting my life experiences with theirs or bring them joy and happiness... The brain will always remember something that caused emotion.

Q. What type of influences derives from your music sound?

A. I say one life a lot because it's my brand and it's self-explanatory. I have different styles of music because you don't need to be put in a box or go by a certain standard. I promote happiness.. to be happy... Nothing less.

Q. Now, I know you have a single titled Insomnia that you released last week for your upcoming project, could you tell us a little about the track and how it came about, and why you chose that to be the single?

A. I have my single Insomnia coming out next week and I chose this song because at a time a lot was going on in my life and I grew from my struggles so I went straightforward tunnel vision with no distractions... it just happened to morph into a turn-up club song so I ran with it.

Q. I heard you had an EP that you're working on that's to be released next year. Could you tell the readers a bit about your EP?

A. Yes, my EP "Lost Files" will be released next year. I write many songs from when I used to produce to more recent. I called it Lost Files because some songs are unreleased tracks that haven't been put out. It's a mix of hype, and slow songs, I have something for everybody in it, ONE LIFE..

Q. Being an upcoming and unsigned artist, what would you say are your biggest challenges you face in the industry?

A. Handling the situations that come with the extreme lifestyle change. I basically had to re-write my moral do's and do not's, and learn how to formerly handle situations with different methods than I've used my entire life.

Q. What current artists do you want to work with in the industry now and why?

A. I would like to work with Daft Punk because I feel like they're able to enhance any art they work on from music to stage performance.

Q. What was the first single you released as an artist and what was the biggest feature you've done so far?

A. The first singe I released was titled "Nirvana" and my biggest feature so far was when I was featured on Yella Montanna's Give Me My Props Album which racked up over twenty million streams.

Q. What do you do in your spare time when you're not doing music?

A. More music, I don't value spare time at this point in my career. If I want to make it, I can't exercise the concept of spare time.

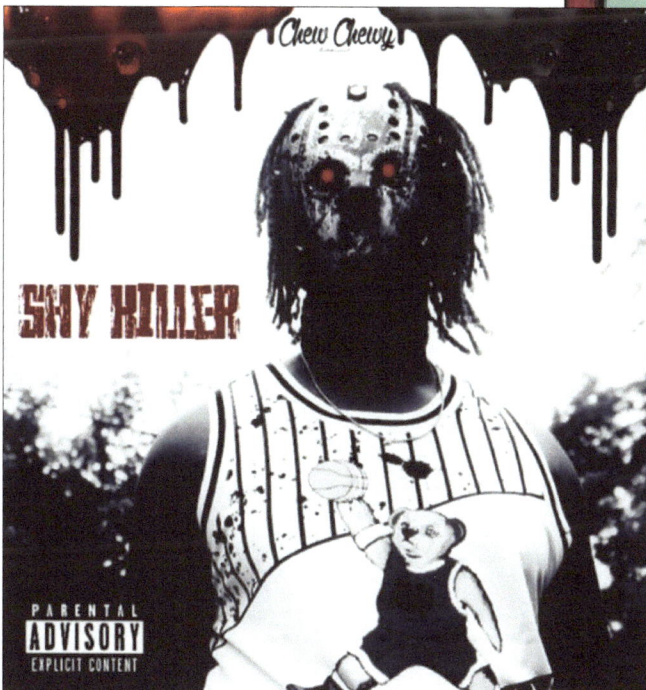

NEXT 2 BLOW
SHY KILLER

SNAP SHOTS

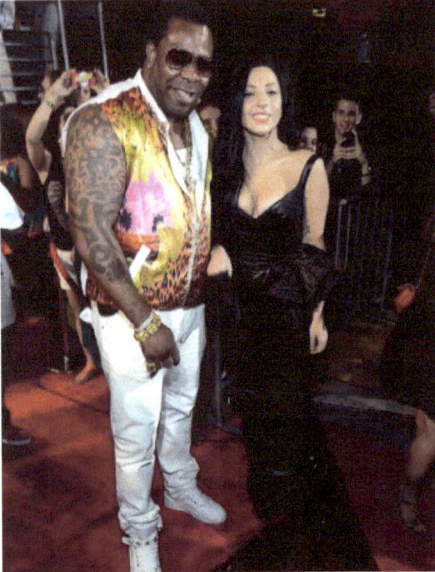

Email Your Snap Shots to
snapshots@sdmlive.com

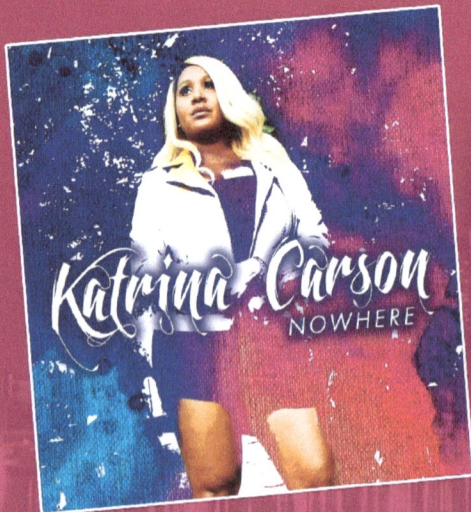

Urban Fiction, Spiritual, Motivation and more.
Order a book from Mocy Publishing today and receive FREE shipping.

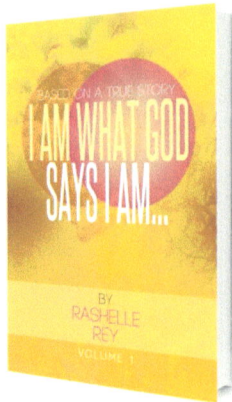

I Am What God Says I Am...
By Rashelle Rey

Item #: IAWGS29
Price: $9.99

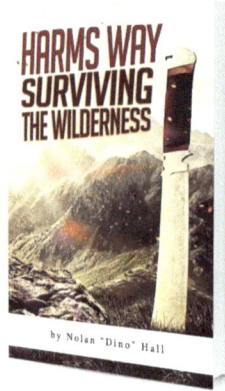

Harm's Way
By Nolan "Dino" Hall

Item #: HWS821
Price: $15.99

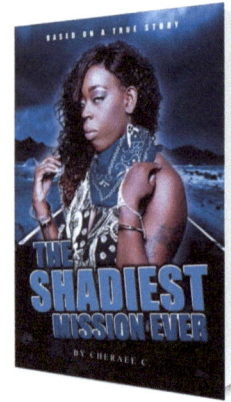

The Shadiest Mission Ever
By Cheraee C.

Item #: TSME28
Price: $12.99

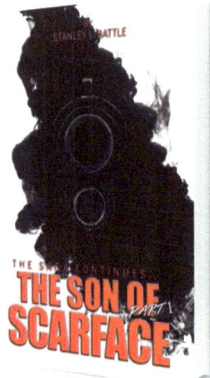

The Son Of Scarface – Part 1
By Stanley L. Battle

Item #: TSOS01
Price: $12.99

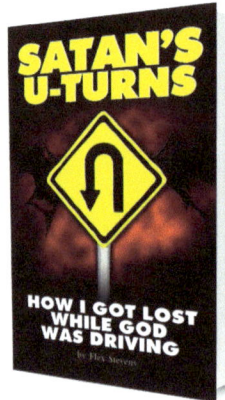

Satan's U-Turns
By Flex Stevens

Item #: SUT382
Price: $9.99

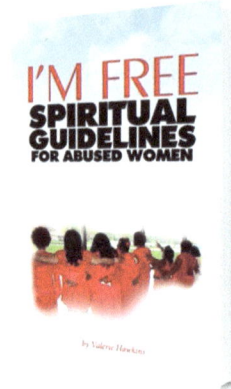

I'm Free
By Valerie Hawkins

Item #: IFTSG82
Price: $14.99

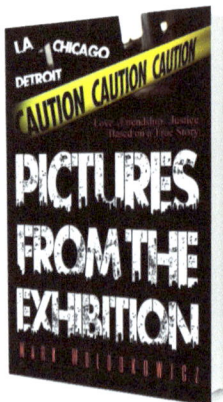

Pictures From The Exhibition
By Mark Wolodkowicz

Item #: PFAE292
Price: $15.99

Behind The Scenes
By Pamela Marshall

Item #: BTS721
Price: $15.99

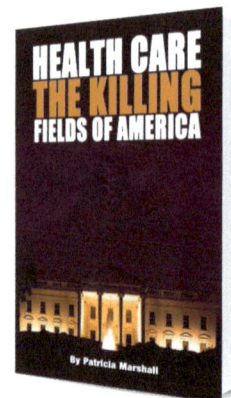

Health Care
By Patricia Marshall

Item #: HCTABF2
Price: $17.99

www.mocypublishing.com
order online and receive FREE shipping. Limit time offer.

REAL MUSIC. REAL ENTERTAINMENT.®

SDM LIVE

ISSUE #19

NEW

Also
K.O.
DUBMUZIK
CROWDFREAK
KING RENIGAD
KADDY REBOS

CARDI B.
THE FEMALES ARE NOW BACK ON TOP OF THE CHARTS WITH HIT MUSIC

WWW.SDMLIVE.COM

BUNNIE
LAUNCHING AN ALL NEW TALK SHOW ON THE SDM NETWORK

www.ingramcontent.com/pod-product-compliance
Lightning Source LLC
Chambersburg PA
CBHW040019050426
42452CB00002B/40